LEARNING
2.0

LEARNING 2.0

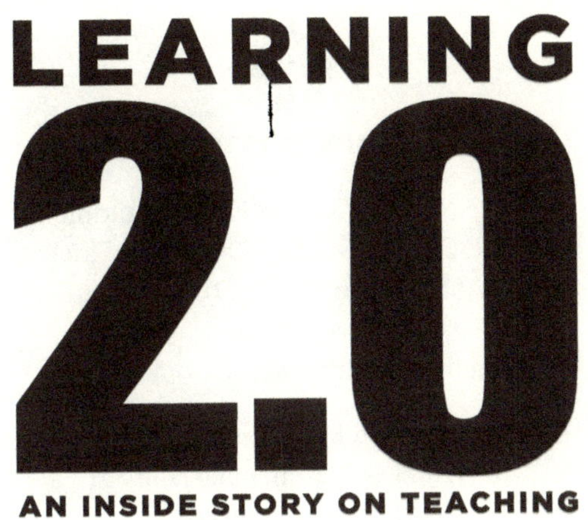

AN INSIDE STORY ON TEACHING

Authored by

MANOJ SONAWANE

penmanbooks.com

Office No. 303, Kumar House Building,
D Block, Central Market, Opp PVR Cinema,
Prashant Vihar, Delhi 110085, India
Website: www.penmanbooks.com
Email: publish@penmanbooks.com

First Published by Penman Books 2019
Copyright © Manoj Sonawane 2019
All Rights Reserved.

Title: Learning 2.0: An Inside Story on Teaching
ISBN: 978-93-89024-30-2

Introduction

Advent of technology has changed the way students perceive the lesson; they will not be interested in your teaching if you just deliver the lesson. They like teachers who not only teaches them but also shows how to learn and perceive lessons, how to present, how to manage, how to leverage course materials, and more. Classes are still conducted uniformly, which should cut down to tailor-made information or courses as per the need of every student to create the knowledge worker, a society needs. It needs a mini setup that provides actual learning experiences, collects the feedbacks and raises drawbacks, but we lack all these in our present educational setup.

Time is running out fast. Old teaching methods are unable to cope with the new changes. On top of that, artificial intelligence is making its way to compete with the human teachers. The communication in teaching is still one-to-many (one-way learning), something that has been failed to create the knowledge worker. Our existing education system is a copy of industrial setup like dress code, hair or nail cut, assembly etc. (factory worker setup) and it still counts the marks in number (think large production figure of the industrial era) rather than a skill.

The rules have changed now. We are at the dawn of the knowledge zenith era where core expertise will sell. In this era your ideas will earn money for you, and you'll not like the idea of your parents who were working for someone else and spending their lifetime to earn fortunes. A worker from the knowledge zenith era will develop core expertise or work on the ideas which will help them to earn the lifetime fortune within few weeks or months. They will prefer learning methods that match or fit them in this knowledge zenith era. Thus, teachers should look for innovative way of learning for this generation and bring it to the classroom.

There are many ways to make learning easy and enjoyable. The first step is to form a story base. We start by building rapport with students by telling them moral, motivational and personal stories which holds the key to bond with them by creating empathy. Make the learning enjoyable by converting textual content into a story or drama. Story weaving and presentation skills are learnable and teachers must develop it by continuous training. Teachers should inculcate the reading habit to create the base for creative story writing and use the same in classroom teaching or learning.

The second key is to create the new content, retain and crystallise it. Be relevant by creating new ideas, set a learning goal to complete it and retain or remember it by applying memory rules.

The third key is learning psychology which provides you a step by step guide to remove the fear of any subject by using Neuro Linguistic Programming (NLP) or reprogram one's mind to learn the hated subject and also build the growth mindset, and manage the content by converting it into a bullet point, mind map or a picture and be confident during the exam by using more of it.

The fourth key is to accelerate the learning by involving students through self-learning process where teachers have to act as mediators and let students learn and act, to encourage the students to use agile ways to simplify the content and help them achieve more in less time and effort by applying leverage or 80/20 principle. Learning creates content, which in turn helps develops knowledge. Let's explore learning 2.0 in a detail.

Contents

PART 3
Learning Psychology

PART 4
Accelerated Learning

PART
One

Learning Through Story

"Tell me the facts and I'll learn. Tell me the truth and I'll believe. But tell me a story and it will live in my heart forever."

—Native American Proverb

CHAPTER
One

Connect Through Story

"After nourishment, shelter, and companionship, stories are the thing we need most in the world."

—*Philip Pullman*

If we allow two enemy kings to seat together and share their life stories, it is likely to end all wars between them. Stories create empathy and connects people with each other. Teachers expects students to listen to them in a class, but don't know how to do this. It's a story that connects teacher with students.

Stories can be powerful as tools. Students like teachers who shares stories with them. Before you embark upon the main content of the topic, you should share a story with students as we are born to interact and express our thoughts, emotions and ideas first. Even a one-minute story is enough to connect with them. You can share small stories on the lines of how you have been inspired to write a poem a few days back and how that poem created a big impact on someone else's life; or share your experience like thrill of climbing a mountain last weekend. Stories may create impact and change personal lives of thousands of students.

How to Create a Story Bank

A teacher should always be prepared to pick up stories from her surroundings and should create story banks and keep them ready for different occasions. She can capture and document stories either in digital form or in a notebook and categorise it in a table as shown below.

Types of Stories	Occasions	Target Audience	Stories
Moral, motivational and personal experiences	Students interaction, student's program etc.	Students	1)...... 2)......
Teaching and learning	Teachers interaction, teacher's programs etc.	Teachers, facilitators	1)...... 2)......
Parenting, childcare	Parents interaction, parent teacher Programs	Parents	1)...... 2)......
Family stories	Family functions or family get together	Family members	1)...... 2)......

Organising your story in the above frame will help you to recall it quickly for any occasion and narrate it to the respective audience. Your story bank would be key to your success. The more stories you have, the more successful you will become. You'll feel more compassionate by using stories from day-to-day life. As John Haidt said, the "human mind is a story processor, not a logic processor". It's a connecting point between two beings.

CHAPTER
Two

How to Convert Educational Topics into Fictional Stories?

Imagine an impact of learning if the study is converted into story and the same is shared with students. Let's consider "Evolution of Mankind" as a topic, for example. In fact, one can convert any topic like this into a fictional story for educational purpose.

Below is a story based on topic Evolution of Mankind.

Evolution of Mankind

Let's use a time machine as a tool to go back to past and explore the evolution of mankind through a story. Tell this story to students in the following way:

> *Let's imagine that we have developed a time machine and want to explore or see the different stages of mankind by using it as a vehicle. Your story starts here:*
>
> *Children, we have three buttons on this time machine – White, Red and Green. The Green button represents the future, Red represents the past and White represents the present. There are three more settings above these buttons representing time – neutral, plus and minus. The plus button can be used to travel to the future and the minus button to the past, while the neutral button setting represents the present. You're going to use white button and neutral time setting to stable the time machine in any time period.*

We are going to the past to see the first stage of mankind, the **Homo Habilis**. *First tune the time setting by pressing the minus button and set the relevant era. Once setting the time, press the Red button to initiate the journey to the past.*

Now the machine starts. You are there, inside it, with the intention to witness the Homo Habilis. Within a few minutes, the machine creates a wormhole in front of it and slowly enters inside. You lose track of time inside the wormhole. After a few more minutes, you find yourself in the era of the homo habilis.

Your machine has landed in a safe place. You have stepped down from it. Now you look around and are surprised to see everything around you and exclaim "How accurate my machine is!" You walk further and find yourself near forage hunter-gatherers but maintain safe distance. As described by your teacher, you are keen to see the features of the Homo Habilis. You observed three main features: first, he could stand on two legs; secondly, there was a slight bend in his spine; and finally, his appearance was similar to apes. For food, they used to hunt small animals and were on constant lookout for eggs, wild fruits and roots. They were using stone choppers as hunting tools. They were barely an improved version of chimpanzees. You record all this information in your notebook.

Now it is time to go back home. You tune the time setting by pressing the plus button and set your current date and time period of earth and click on Green button to take you to the future. The machine operates the same way, entering in the wormhole to go to the future. Within a few minutes, you reach the present period.

Now you are more excited and wanted to explore the other past forms of the human species. You decide to travel to the period of **Homo Erectus**.

Next day, you are set to prepare yourself for next adventure. You go near time machine in the backyard of your home. You step inside and sit calmly. Various thoughts pop up inside your mind. You ask yourself: what if my time machine fails or is unable to return present time? What I will do there in Homo Erectus period in that case? Should I help them by informing about present-day technological advancements?

Eventually you shake your head and ignore these thoughts and initiate the operation of time machine by applying same operating rules as last time. Within a few minutes you reach the relevant period. Rather than stepping down from the time machine, you decided to fly it in the sky and observe this period from above. You suddenly see a band of hunter-gatherers running down on the African Savannah. They do not notice you in the sky. You take out lenses to observe them. They are different from the Homo Habilis. They stood erect like present human beings, which is why they are called Homo Erectus. They used symmetrical tools, like axes, for hunting. They used them to cut and eat calorie-dense meat and marrow to fuel their brain growth. Another group was eating honey, tubers, berries and baobab fruit. You observe that their brains are more developed as they were eating more nutritious food to fuel their brain growth. You note down all this in your diary.

After observing all this you decided to move to present time. You return to your backyard where you land your time machine safely.

The second time travelling had been much more adventurous than the first, as you had observed things more clearly, from the sky. The experience of watching mankind in its initial stages has been thrilling for you. Now you are set for your third and last time travel.

On early morning on a Sunday, you plan to see the **Neanderthals***. You have heard a lot about them as they were near-ancestors of the* **Homo Sapiens***.*

You wake up early in the morning on Sunday. You walk towards the backyard. It is 6 AM. You decide to return by 9 AM. You are a 10-year-old child in the year 2091. The lesson on the evolution of mankind had been taught in your class last week. You have borrowed this time machine from another time traveller who happened to be from a different planet. She had been exploring our planet and were agreed to lend you the machine for a few days as you helped her to know life on planet earth. She was a guest on planet earth for a few weeks and had been travelling and exploring the planet using teleportation. She belonged to an advanced civilisation. She was about to take back her time machine by Sunday evening.

You are near the time machine. You think about that alien lady. She is like a god, and has many advanced tools compared to human beings. She has conquered death and has been living for thousands of years. She has been doing interstellar travel for many years.

You set the time machine. As usual it vanishes from home backyard and reaches to the period of the Neanderthals. This time you find yourself in Europe. After landing at safe place, you step out of the machine and walk towards a Neanderthal camp. It is cold out there. There is a fire outside the camp, which means that the Neanderthals are familiar with the art of making fire. You walk further to see their tools and observe them clearly. They used the spear, the hand axe and large pebbles very tactfully, which indicates that they are more intelligent than Homo Habilis and Homo Erectus. They look big and strong in physical appearance. They are hunting large animals. Meat, plants and some herbs are main source of their diet. You note down all this in your notebook.

After this expedition, you set to return home. You look at your wristwatch. It was 8.55.35 AM. You know that the watch was showing current time of earth. You set time 8.55.35 AM on Sunday, 13 May 2091. You return home in a few minutes.

> *You enter the corridor of your home through backyard. While walking, you peep inside the kitchen, where your mother is preparing the Sunday breakfast. Your younger brother and father are still sleeping in their respective bedrooms. None of them is aware of your adventure and about that secret time machine you kept in the backyard.*
>
> *You are completely moved by this adventure as you have encountered not only three stages of mankind but five, including the present-day civilisation and the time traveller from the distant planet who has already achieved godlike feats. You are relaxed and sit on the couch thinking about the evolution of mankind from an Animal like human to god like lady alien.*

You can convert many such chapters or topics into stories by using a story weaving skill.

CHAPTER
Three

How to Develop Story Weaving and Presentation Skills?

"It's like everyone tells a story about themselves inside their own head. Always. All the time. That story makes you what you are. We build ourselves out of that story."

—Patrick Rothfuss

Developing story weaving skills among students by a librarian or a teacher will be an additional asset for the professional, as imparting such a skill will help the students to emerge as creative writers or authors. All writers or authors have these skills knowingly or unknowingly as most books are based on stories, whether fiction or experience-based writing (non-fiction). Story weaving skills help anyone to create content. Librarians and teachers love the books. With proper training, they can easily attain the expertise in story weaving skill.

Stories can be broadly divided into two parts

1. Fictional stories
2. Non-fictional stories

Fictional Stories

Most of the children have inborn ability to create a story instantly. They live a life in the moment and make a story based on the situation. As they grow older, they lose story-weaving skills because of not practicing it. If encouraged, children can turn into authors or writers at an early age. Give them situations, and they can weave plots around them quickly. Forget plots, ask them to weave a story around random words; to your surprise they will create a story. Let's discuss how to do this:

How to Weave Fictional Stories

The librarian or the teacher must conduct **Story-Weaving Activity** based on any random word. Involve students from both primary and secondary grade sections for this activity. It is a fun-filled classroom activity where classroom rows are numbered 1, 2, 3 and 4 or whatever maximum number of rows of the classroom. Each row gets a word from another row in the same classroom. Below is the activity detail.

1. Row 1 gets a random word from Row 2,

2. Row 2 gets a random word from Row 3,

3. Row 3 gets a random word from Row 4,

4. Row 4 gets a random word from Row 1

The librarian or the teacher may facilitate this activity by assigning scores or points to the row for weaving one-minute stories around the random word. For example, if Row 1 gets the word "box" from Row 2, then any child from Row 1 will raise the hand to weave a story around "box". The representative child of that Row (1) will have to create a one-minute story around that word instantly and tell it to the whole class. If done, points will be awarded by the librarian or the teacher to that row. Likewise, every row gets a word to weave a story around it based on the above activity details. The final score and winner row would be announced once the activity gets over. It will surprise you that based on our research in a particular school, every student was able to weave a story around any random word and the score was always equal for every row.

Many fictional stories can be created by using this activity in a single class and this skill would be useful for students in developing essay writing skill for any language.

Non-Fictional Stories

Non-fictional stories are often based on experience from life or profession. One can easily weave story if they are based on personal experiences because they remember them in detail and retain it for long periods of time. Irrespective of whether they are derived from life or business, stories should always consist of setup, struggle and success. Struggle forms an important part in this framework. No struggle, no story, they say, and human beings love to know about the sufferings of others.

How to Weave Non-Fictional Stories

Suppose you have a story that includes the above-mentioned frames that is setup, struggle and success. Find a corner and write down your ready-to-share story. Give it a title. Below is an example of a story titled *Hindi Medium*, based on life experience.

> ### Hindi Medium
>
> *I remember it was Monday. My mother and I left home early in the morning. I was walking with her, unaware of*

our destination. After about ten minutes we reached near one of the buildings. I saw some children playing on the ground. They were playing a game, singing a song "fire in the jungle, run, run! Fire in the jungle, run, run!" I was curious, but my mother didn't allow me to stand and watch. We entered a building, where she enquired about the Principal's office.

We waited outside the office for our turn to enter for admission inquiry. My mother seemed anxious. She must have been thinking about my admission in the school. We were allowed to enter after half an hour. He offered us seats. My mother started the conversation and requested for my admission, but her dreams were shattered when she got the typical reply of "admissions are full in our school".

She requested the Principal to do something. "My son's year will be wasted if he does not get admission. There is hardly any school in this area except this one," she told him.

But he refused to do anything. We left his cabin without hope. As we walked down a corridor, she suddenly said, "let's meet Aaji (Grandma)." Aaji, Kerubai Bhosle, was the mother of Karuna, a neighbour and friend of my mother. She used to work as support staff in that school.

Aaji soon came to meet us there in the corridor. She was our last hope. My mother told her everything. Aaji told her, "Why are you insisting on admission in

Marathi medium section of this school when education is the same in both Hindi and Marathi mediums? I work here as support staff in the Hindi medium section. As per my knowledge admissions are available readily in that section. Let's meet the Hindi medium section Principal".

She also informed us that I could switch from Hindi to Marathi medium next year if she wanted to. Though my mother tongue is Marathi, my mother agreed to her suggestion and was happy about me not having to lose an academic year. She got me admitted to the Hindi medium section; that was where my education journey started.

Initially faced a language barrier but soon adapted to the new language. Next year my mother didn't get my section changed. I completed my Secondary School Certificate from Hindi medium section.

After passing school, I took admission in a college and got enrolled in the science stream. The language of instruction in college was English. I remember my first day in college. It was a feeling similar to mine in Grade 1 after I was admitted to the Hindi medium section: a six-year-old boy who had never heard Hindi was clueless about that language.

The students from English-medium schools had an advantage compared to vernacular-medium students like me. They asked questions and discussed problems with the facilitator in English. I made up my mind. I decided *that by the time I completed my HSC (10+2) I would be fluent in English.*

However, once you decide to improve on something you actually have to resolve various aspects of that problem. I asked questions like "How to learn English?" "How to be fluent in English?" and "What to do to have command over the English language?"

In response, I got answers on the lines of "read English newspapers", "watch English movies and news channels", "always talk in English with your friends," etc. I followed them consistently. They worked. By the time I passed HSC, I was speaking in English and had command over the Language. I overcame the language barrier second time in my life.

English helped me complete my B.Sc., M.Sc. and M.L.I.Sc. (Master of Library and Information Science). It remains a prized possession till today. This language is helping me do business at International level and earn money.

The above story has all ingredients of framework. The **Setup**: ground, school, principal cabin, corridor, college etc. The **Struggle**: to gain admission in school and break the barrier to speak in Hindi and English. And the **Success**: getting admission in Hindi medium school, overcome the language barrier and completed his education.

How to present non-fictional stories in front of the audience

Once your story is ready, share it with the audience. Following is the contemporary presentation skill.

Once your name is called upon a stage, walk towards the stage with a little energy. Next, look into the eyes of the host while shaking the hand and touch the elbow slightly and thanking the host (in other words, taking over the stage from the host). Then stand at the centre of the stage by making the steeple hand and pan the audience for three to five second (power pause). Always open your talk by using three sentences: 1) I remember, 2) Imagine and 3) Your direct question to the audience, like "have you gone through the pain of losing the money in share market?" After this, start a talk on main content. You can use two more hand poses during a talk: the power pose and the beggar's hand.

End your talk by giving it a signature end (signature end means bringing out the core from your talk and giving a message to the audience. Never ever say these sentences at the end: 1) I hope you liked my talk 2) I hope you enjoyed my session or 3) How many of you liked this speech?

Your story should release all three hormones: cortisol, dopamine and oxytocin. Cortisol will create an attention (when you use the words "I remember", the audience will start thinking, what does the presenter remember?).

Dopamine will keep the audience hooked and make them curious to know what is next (you can release this hormone by providing vivid details of your story, for example, Monday morning, walking on the road and children singing the song in above story). Oxytocin is the hormone that makes your audience emotional and connects heart to heart. They are also known as love hormones (in above story, the mother's struggle to get her child admitted in school, child facing language barrier etc can be cited as examples).

The same may be applicable to business stories as well where you use the same framework – setup, struggle and success of your business to connect with the audience and share your business experience in a story form. Thus, the above framework is a contemporary communication or presentation skill where you connect to your audience with the stories.

Teachers can use many insights of contemporary presentation skills in classroom teaching like showing some energy while entering inside the class, pan the students for three to five second before teaching (power pause), using steeple hand while standing, power pose when high on learning and beggar's hand for evaluating the learning outcome.

CHAPTER
Four

Reading Habit: A Base for Creative Story Writing

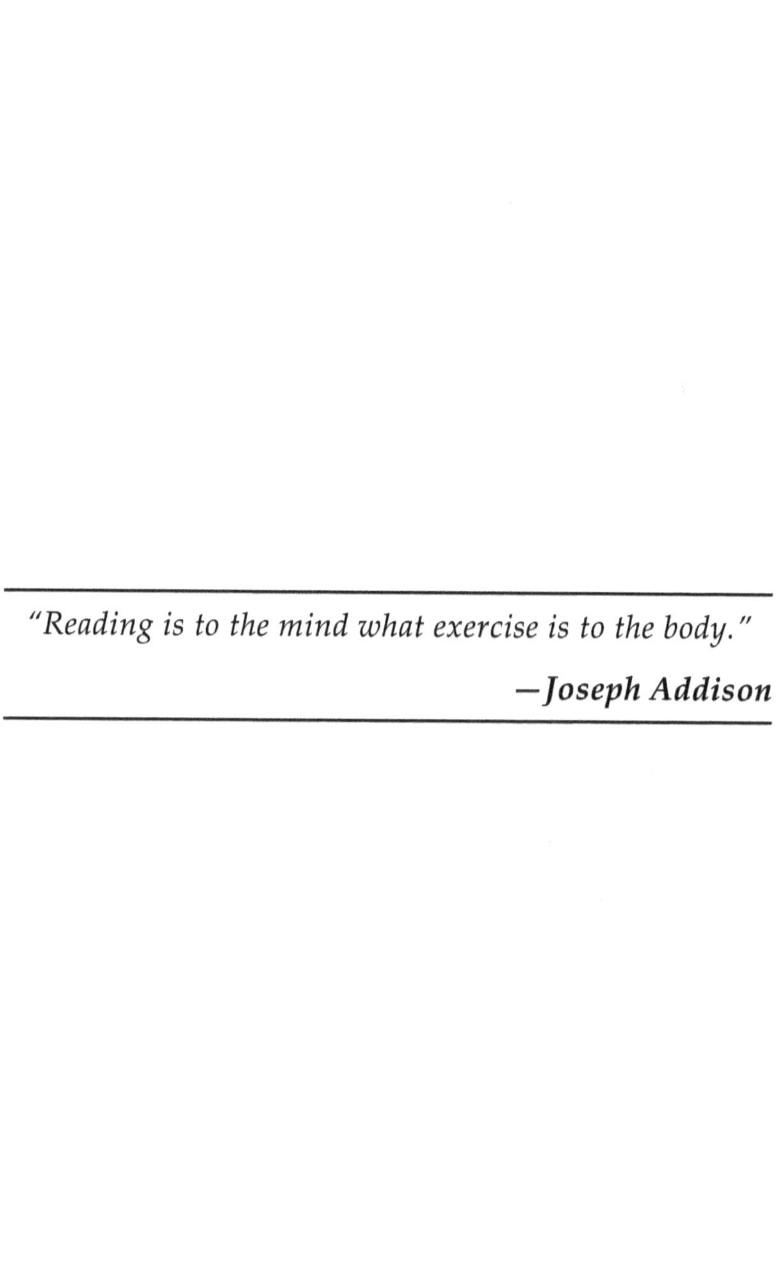

"Reading is to the mind what exercise is to the body."
—Joseph Addison

Books play an important role in learning and create many great stories but often we hear from students or parents that barring a few, they don't have time to read books (and grow rich in the process). Here is a way to read more and more books:

If you're watching television or surfing the internet two to three hours a day, you can reduce this time by an hour a day to save 365 hours an year. If you divide that by forty-hour work week, you'll see that you'll have added about nine-and-a-half additional weeks of productivity to your life. That is two additional months every year! Use this additional hour to read books of motivation, education, training and self-esteem. It's sure that it will make a profound difference in your life.

If you're not ok with one hour for daily reading, just keep aside 15 minutes a day. In fact, you can read a book a month –which amounts to 12 books a year – by reading only 15 minutes every day. Here's how:

The average high school students read 250 words a minute. But we all stop to re-read a sentence from time to time... or pause to think about a new idea. So it's fair to say that the average reading rate for the most of adults 200 words a minute.

There are about 400 words on an average book page, which means the average reader should be able to read it in two minutes. At this rate, you can read seven pages in a 15-minute period.

Suppose there are 210 pages in an average book. So, by reading 15 minutes (seven pages) a day, you can read the book in 30 days. It may take you more than a month to read longer books, but by and large if you read 15 minutes a day, you'll be able to finish a book a month.

By the end of the year, you'll have read at least 12 books. By the end of 10 years, that will add up to 120 books! Just think, by setting aside just 15 minutes a day, you can easily read 120 books that may help you grow richer in all aspects of life. By doubling your daily reading time to just half an hour, you can read 25 books a year – 250 books in 10 years.

That's why one should not be sympathetic with people who say that **they don't have the time to read and grow rich**. That's nonsense. They have the time. They're just choosing to use their time doing something they value more than reading.

How to imprint thought on importance of reading?

Reading plays an important role in learning. One has to imprint the importance of reading on a child's mind at a tender age. Mental imprint process helps us to instil the importance of reading on child's mind. For this, one can create a poster of different messages or thoughts on reading by great thinkers or philosophers and paste it on a wall at home or any prominent place and read it on a daily basis for 21 days to imprint it on the child's mind. Following are the examples of messages on reading and books by great thinkers.

1. *Our life changes in two ways through the people we meet and the books we read. –* **Harvey Mackay**

2. *You cannot live fully in mind without books. –* **Napoleon Hill**

3. *If we encounter a man of rare intellect, we should ask him what books he reads. –* **Ralph Waldo Emerson**

4. *Reading is to the mind what exercise is to the body. –* **Joseph Addison**

5. *All Great Leaders Are Readers. –* **Unknown**

There are many such thoughts on reading by great thinkers available on internet and in books. Compile these, make a poster of it and paste it on wall. The child must see the poster every day. This is the easiest way to convey the message on importance of reading books. Inculcating a reading habit helps to create the base for creative story writing.

PART
Two

Content Creation, Retention and Crystallisation

> *"It is the supreme art of the teacher to awaken joy in creative expression and knowledge."*
>
> **—Albert Einstein**

CHAPTER
Five

How to Create Content

*"Writing is an extreme privilege but it's also a gift.
It's a gift of giving a story to someone."*

—Amy Tan

You might have heard about many tools to make life better. These are called **tools for life**. On a similar note, we have tools for developing content. These are called **tools to create content**, which helps us crystallise our thoughts. Apart from notebooks and modern gadgets, we will discuss about most effective creative tools in this chapter. These tools play an important role as they create fresh ideas or content for the world. Let's discuss below:

Sticky Notes as Learning Tool

For example, authors use sticky notes to write down titles of different plots and stick them in their studios. They influence the author to create conversations among character of that plot. This way, the author finds it easy to finish plots and put them in necessary sequence to eventually complete her fictional work. Learning through sticky notes helps the author to connect the dots and create a full picture out of nowhere.

Books as a Learning Tool

Take the example of Hollywood or Bollywood story writers who use books as learning tools. They are mostly inspired by national and international books to construct plotlines for their movies. Here is how they do it.

They develop fiction or real-life story collection of books on various genres. This phase is called Collection Development. Suppose they want to write a story on a crime mystery, they will read the best books on this genre from their collection which in turn will help them to form new stories inspired from these books. Here, too, they use books as learning tools to develop content.

Blackboards as a Learning Tool

Apart from using sicky notes and books to develop the new content, many people use blackboards or whiteboards as learning tools at home or work. It is a simple and widely used tool to write down ideas, and is considered among the most effective and creative as well, because if an idea pops up in your mind, you can write it down immediately on the board to create a picture of your idea on such huge board. Your written idea or picture will help you develop and elaborate the content further. You can relate different topics to each other by using it. You can also teach your child by using a board as they are mentally wired to learn through it. You can also train them to write down or draw pictures of their ideas on boards at home.

Learning tools like sticky notes headlines, books and black board plays an important role in developing new content. It is not only used by author or strategist but also by scientist to formulate the concept, develop the formula or logic the equation.

CHAPTER
Six

Content Retention by Applying Senses

> *"True alchemy lies in this formula: your memory and your senses are but the nourishment of your creative impulse."*
>
> *—Arthur Rimbaud*

VAK (Visual, Auditory and Kinaesthetic)

Usage of visual, auditory and kinaesthetic senses helps you to achieve learning goals quickly. Let's use these senses in learning of below words. You have to remember all 13 words in sequence by using visual, auditory and kinaesthetic senses.

1. Book
2. Pen
3. Car
4. Hill
5. Lion
6. Lake
7. Hritik
8. Mangoes
9. Giraffe
10. Bus
11. School
12. Salman
13. Cold drink

Remembering all these 13 words in sequence by using rote method is tedious job. You tended to forget the sequence after a few days. However, you will remember it easily and can retain it for a longer time if you weave a story around these words by use of visual, auditory and kinaesthetic senses. Let's create a story first:

"I have a red colour **book** with a picture of a **pen** on it and I kept it inside the blue **car**. I drove the car to a **hill** and came across a **lion** over there who ordered me to cross the **lake**. While crossing it, I met **Hritik** who, while dancing next to the lake, offered me **mangoes**. I like the sweet taste of mangoes and drove further and then came across a huge **giraffe** walking on the road, I caught the giraffe and put it inside the **Bus**. The bus went to the **school** and stopped at the gate where **Salman** was offering a **cold drink** to everyone nearby".

Visual Senses

You are using **visual senses** in above story by putting pictures, colours, applying weird concepts, connecting listed words with each other like a garland. We can add as many words as we want and can keep on weaving a story. You'll not forget a single word from the list.

Auditory Senses

You will apply the auditory senses if you tell the above story to someone or yourself, which will help you have a further firm grip in your mind.

Kinaesthetic Senses

You apply kinaesthetic senses if you write the above story and practice it on notebook. Applying all the senses in learning helps us to achieve learning goal.

How to use this method in actual learning

Now let's take the goal of leaning or practicing this skill for converting chapters, concepts or paragraphs into stories. You can practise this skill on complex topics that we hear or learn it first time. For example, you can apply this method to remember the brain frequency like Delta (~0.1- 4 Hz), Theta (~4 - 7 Hz), Alpha (~7 - 13 Hz) and Beta (~13 - 30 Hz) in ascending order by converting it into a story, here is a story of brain frequency:

"Delta is a fat boy who asked Theta, why are you so thin? Theta says, I go to Alpha classes where Beta beats me a lot. That's why I am thin."

It's a small and one sentence story but helps us to remember brain frequency in ascending order for longer time. You can practise this skill on several concepts or topics as human brain never forget the content if converted into story. Develop this skill by applying it on many topics.

CHAPTER
Seven

Content Crystallisation by Setting Goals

> *"The people who get things done, who lead, who grow and who make an impact…those people have goals."*
>
> **—Seth Godin**

It is well-known that those with goals are successful and those without are not. Setting a goal is an important exercise for everyone, whether you are teacher, students, businessman or doctor. A goal helps us to achieve more in less time. If you have ten things to complete in next ten days, it means that you have one day for each of job. You get clarity once you set a schedule. In this chapter we shall focus on learning goals of teachers and students.

Breathing in Learning

We have heard that venture capitalists fund their companies for expansion and hiring of best talent from industries to make more money. Such funding is called a breathing fund for a business to survive. Time is equivalent to fund in learning and giving more time to learn a particular subject means giving more breathing to it.

Vacations are the best time for teachers and students to learn or to give breathing to any subject. You can set your learning goal during vacations. It may include goals like learning grammar or practicing base formulas in mathematics, preparing mind maps of lengthy chapters, converting answer in vertical form etc.

Preparing your learning sessions in advance will help you ascertain prominent questions of the chapters or unresolved issues of the chapters and can be considered as identified goal (i.e. preparing for the session). Now, there is a gap between the questions you have and the answers you seek. Your mind starts to fill this gap or wants to close this open loop as soon as possible. Open loops are unresolved issues or goals that need to be identified and put it in a scheduled program to command your mind to accomplish it.

How to close the open loop or unresolved issues or unfinished goals

If you have identified unresolved issues or open loops or unfinished goals and want to close it in a definite timeline, write down the same in a tabular form.

Suppose your summer vacation starts from 1st May and ends on 11th June. You have a total of 42 days to accomplish your goals. Prioritise the goal as per your urgency. Remember, you have to finish one goal at a time. If you have set 42 days to finish seven goals, you get six days on an average to finish each goal. Some goals may take longer time and some may be finished early, but by and large you are entitled to accomplish it within the specified time limit. Remember that investing your time wisely is key to your success and goals help you manage it appropriately.

Things I must do in next 42 days, i.e., not later than 11th June 2019, 12.00 AM

Create the list of "**Agile Math Formulas**" and categorise it chapter wise.
Learn the agile way of creating **Math table between 12-99 and practise it.**
Write down the three "**Fictional Stories**" to sharpen the English writing skill.
Finish **reading of 10 books** from the wish list reads.
Learn and practise the skills of **converting chapter, concepts or paragraph into stories.**
Convert all the complex subject chapters into **Mind Map, tabulation, flow chart and vertical form.**
Watch **30 educational videos** related to my subject learning

CHAPTER
Eight

Content Crystallisation Through Sleep

> *"Even a soul submerged in sleep is hard at work and helps make something of the world."*
>
> **—Heraclitus**

To get this book out of my head and to write it in an MS Word file, I have been required to follow two rules. The first was to follow a deep work philosophy; and secondly, I ensured I had proper sleep between three to seven in the morning (creative writing sleep). A deep work philosophy means isolating yourself from your daily routine for one to two weeks and focusing on knowledge task for example writing article or book or learning any new skills like communication skill. Secondly, having sound sleep between three to seven is of utmost importance for language writing skills, which includes framing the sentence or paragraph and thinking creatively for content. Let us discuss how:

It is scientifically proved that our sleep is divided into four stages at night viz. Stage I, II, III and IV. If a person feels sleepy and go to bed at 11 PM, her initial sleep state is called as stage I level sleep; then it slowly moves to stage II, then III and IV. Stages III and IV are deep sleep; this lasts from 11 PM to 3 AM. After three, the sleep level switches back to stage II, which remains constant till 7 in the morning. Stage I level sleep is waking up or the state of feeling sleepy. Now let's discuss the significance of stages II, III and IV level sleep:

Importance of Stage III and IV level Sleep or Deep Sleep (11 PM to 3 AM Sleep)

Sleep stages III and IV are most valuable for retaining hard facts, names, dates, formulas, and concepts. This makes it most important for history and geography papers, where one has to remember a lot of dates, names, facts etc. If you're preparing for a test that's heavy on retention like foreign vocabulary or chemical structure, it's better to get the full dose of deep sleep and roll out of bed early for a quick review.

Importance of Stage II level Sleep (3.00 AM to 7.00 AM Sleep)

Sleep stage II consolidates motor skills that is useful for rhythmic body movement and synchronisation (or it helps an athlete to control and balance body movement). You may lose the athletic competition if you wake up at three in the morning and practise the move as you have missed stage II, which has impacted your motor skills. The goal of winning in the athletic competition can be achieved only by having a proper sleep between three to seven in the morning.

Sleep stage II is also most valuable for creative thinking in mathematics and science, language writing skill or creative writing, formulation of concepts and designing molecular structure.

I am using stage II level sleep to write this book. This level sleep has helped me to develop the content for this book, think creatively, frame the sentences, lines, paragraphs etc.

All of this to say that if you're going to burn the candle, it helps to have some idea of which end to burn.

PART
Three

Learning Psychology

"The only person who is educated is the one who has learned how to learn and change."

—**Carl Rogers**

CHAPTER
Nine

Neuro Linguistic Programming (NLP) for Study

"Change the way you look at things and the things you look at change."

—*Wayne W. Dyer*

How to Use NLP in Study

Have you ever thought why you wear what you wear? You had loved a type of dress at some point. When it came to buying, you ended up buying the same type of dress. A similar rule is applicable to studying. You love to study particular subjects – ones you like most - and end up knowing more about it. Loving a subject is similar to loving a kind of dress as your mind tricks you to make the different kind of choices in a love-or-hate pattern. It provides priority to the things you like or love most. All other unwanted aspects, including subjects you hate most, are filtered out. You stop receiving more information about it, which may affect your exams. In such cases, you need to reprogram your mind or break this pattern. The process of breaking old patterns is called as Neuro Linguistic Programming or NLP.

Steps to break the old pattern:

Step 1. Create a new vision of your study goal. Use the sentence in present tense as our brain perceives everything as now.

Step 2. Create powerful declarations and affirmations that support that new vision.

Step 3. Develop emotional anchors for neural linking.

Step 4. Prepare a portfolio of imprinting material

Step 5. Maintain a brief daily routine of reconditioning techniques three times a day (after waking up, at midday, before bed)

All these steps are elaborated below for your reference.

NLP Steps:

Step 1: Vision

1. My total marks in a mathematics is 100 out of 100 (or whatever the maximum possible score is)

Step 2: Affirmation

1. I love to teach or learn mathematics anytime.
2. Mathematics is a scoring subject.
3. I am a genius at mathematics
4. Everyone is helping me to be an expert in mathematics.

Step 3: Neural Linking

Linking the solid example for your affirmation is called as Neural linking. For example, neural linking for the affirmation **I am a genius in mathematics"** is given below:

"I was in a complete control while solving the mathematics problem on my classroom board. I received admiration from my friends and teachers. I was admired as "a genius in mathematics". This helps you to make that statement true in real sense." You can take any incidence like this to make the neural linking.

Step 4: Prepare your neural imprinting material

Laminate your vision. Use a vision board where you can paste pictures of your future achievements, like your photo holding the play card of sentence "My total marks in Mathematics is 100 out of 100" and look at this photo thrice daily, in the morning, at midday, and before bedtime.

Step 5: Neural Reconditioning Process

Do the following thrice a day, in the morning, at midday, and before bedtime. Follow the below steps in sequence.

1. Meditations: Close your eyes and concentrate in the centre of your two eyes. Do not think for at least ten minutes. Calm your mind.

2. Visualisations: Run a moving picture of your goals or vision in your mind.

3. Affirmation: Write or declare the affirmation as per your need. Examples are given above.

It is guaranteed that after 21 days you will feel change and will subsequently achieve speedy success at Mathematics.

It is clear from above that you have given a priority to mathematics by using NLP. You have also broken the hate pattern of your brain for mathematics. Mathematics falls under the category of things you love most.

Now your brain gives priority to mathematics and diverts your attention to the things important to the mathematics and helps you improve on it. Earlier you were ignoring it due to a hate pattern for mathematics. You have reprogrammed your brain wiring to like your most-hated subject. You can use this for any other subject.

CHAPTER
Ten

How We Learn

"Teaching children is an accomplishment; getting children excited about learning is an achievement."

—Robert John Meehan

How to make a studying interesting? To answer this question, one has to understand the psychology behind it. We need a flow to help us focus on anything. Flow embarks the deep work. One can see a flow when a child plays a mobile or video games. Children show interest in games. Interest initiates a flow, which, in turn, pushes the child to deep work – in this case, playing a game. Once there, she can play video games for hours and hours, as the interest has transcended to flow and then to deep work. She does things not by force but by choice. Choices initiate the interest at this stage. Similarly, she can learn to study by choice and not by force. Many parents behave in the exact opposite and apply force.

How We Learn?

Before knowing how we learn, one should ask why a child is ready to play the game at any point of time but she behaves the exact opposite when it comes to studying. The answer is that child plays a game by choice, thus setting her brain frequency in alpha mode. Alpha mode is the conscious frequency of the brain that helps to play games or to learn. This frequency will be available to her if she chooses to study through choice.

Now we need to know how to make learning a choice. Yes, there are ways for it. Remember, when we were in school, we loved to read vertical content more than horizontal. We prefer to convert content to bullet points or mind maps or pictures. One can convert whole chapters into single pages by using mind maps. The best way to prepare for examinations is to learn the mind map technique.

CHAPTER
Eleven

Growth Mindset

Building a growth mindset doesn't mean providing positive environment to your child or praising for her achievements. Growth mindset creates new opportunities and believes in learning new things or accept changes, raising drawbacks and always setting new challenges. Praise and positive environment are temporary, whereas building challenging environment and teaching children to overcome are permanent and are key to build the growth mindset.

The reason behind this is that our forage hunter-gatherer ancestors faced many challenges in the past while walking through the jungle and had to find ways to overcome them, keeping survival (growth mindset) at the same time. Praises and positive environments are relatively recent phenomenon. Questioning on drawbacks and providing feedback are essential to building the growth mindset.

How to use it in learning setup

Before teaching any topic, teachers have to frame questions and problems on that topic and ask students to solve them. This is similar to providing them with challenges to overcome. This should be done for every topic. Let them seek the answer before they are taught. Here is how it works:

1. Select the chapter, frame questions or problems and hand them over to the students.

2. Ask the students to prepare on that topic before you actually teach them.

3. Begin the teaching once all of them are done with the self-preparatory exercise regarding the questions or the problems.

4. Measure the learning impact.

The teacher will act as a mediator in learning. Learning of the topic will be more impactful as compared to old teaching ways where teachers used to teach first and provide exercises only upon completion. Let's examine the importance of self-preparation by using the jackfruit story below.

Jackfruit Story

A group of forage hunter-gatherers was passing through the jungle and they found a strange tree bearing strange fruits. They are not sure whether the fruits are edible or poisonous, but they have to evaluate that to overcome their hunger. Jack, leader of the band, decided to try first. He ate it and found the pulp of this fruit sweet and very tasty. The other group members followed his example and tasted this new fruit. They decided to name it jackfruit, in honour of Jack. Jackfruit now became a common fruit for this group.

Now, another group of forage hunger-gatherers was passing through the same jungle. They saw the jackfruit tree for the first time. However, a man standing below the tree informed the group members its name and offered the group to eat this new variety of fruit. The whole group accepted this offer and ate it. After finishing the fruit they moved on to next jungle.

The first group will remember it for a longer period of time. They will remember its shape, size, smell, textures etc. as they had overcome the hunger problem by themselves and had also christened the fruit. They can recognise this fruit anywhere in the jungle. The second group, on the other hand, had the information regarding that fruit readily. Next time, even though they will pass through a jackfruit tree in another jungle, they may not recognise it as they had hardly any association with the tree or fruit.

In the above example the man standing below the jackfruit tree is similar to a teacher using old teaching methods, who fed information students could hardly associate with.

We should let the students learn and act. We will discuss about same in the next section.

PART
Four

Accelerated Learning

"*Tell me and I'll forget. Show me and I may remember. Involve me and I learn.*"

—Benjamin Franklin

CHAPTER
Twelve

Teach to Act

"Nothing will work unless you do."

—**Maya Angelou**

Rules have been changed at the rise of knowledge society where teachers have to act as a mediator and let the students learn & act. Students are born to act. Action involves them. Here are some self-learning methods:

1. One-to-one learning and

2. Group learning process.

One-to-one Learning

Let the students learn by using one-to-one learning methods. The process involves following steps:

1. Teacher select a few learners and trains them on a chapter

2. Each of these learners trained by teacher will teach it to at least one student

3. Now, the next trained group will follow the same and will teach it at least one student

4. The process will continue till the time we finish one-to-one-learning for whole class

5. At the end teacher will reflect or summarise the chapter for whole class to control any wrong teaching

Students learn better when they teach it to someone. It helps them to prepare on their own. As discussed in the previous chapter they fall under the category of group number one of forage hunter-gatherers and provide importance to self-preparation or learning.

Group Learning

Learning content from each other using group learning method involves the following steps:

1. A topic has been assigned to an individual group

2. The topic is further broken down in subtopics depending on the number of individuals

3. Each individual will prepare for the given subtopic

4. They will share subtopics with each other and complete the learning of whole topic together

5. In whole process teacher just act as a mediator and help them to prepare the right frame of learning.

You can see that it will be easier for them to prepare for subtopics. At the same time, they will learn better from each other. One-to-one learning or group learning methods help students to learn better from their friend as compared to the teacher. Learning output is high in one-to-one learning and group learning methods as the command is given to students by teachers.

How to implement interactive teaching and sprint learning methods

Interactive teaching: Studies have shown that interactive teachers hook students better to learning when compared to one-way learning process. Here's a way to be interactive. If you have a 30-minute class, divide the topic in three parts. Change the term when you move from one part of a topic to another. Changing the term involves asking students to repeat important core points of the current part of a topic together before moving on to the next part. Alternately, ask them to give a hi-five to each other; while doing this, ask them to exchange motivational sentences on the lines of "You're awesome!", "You're intelligent!" Or "You're a genius!" etc. This makes the class interactive.

Sprint Learning: Consider a subject containing ten chapters for a test. Learning all chapters at the same time doesn't make any sense. Divide the 10 chapters into 10 parts and allot timeline for each one. Here, each chapter is a sprint (a piece of work must be completed). Working on a sprint is easier than on working on everything at the same time just before the exam. Learning one sprint at a time is like eating a small piece of a meal at a time for better digestion. Mapping all subjects and planning at the beginning of the year will help you sprint. Guide the students on sprint learning, planning or goal setting.

CHAPTER
Thirteen

Agile Way of Learning

"There's a way to do it better-find it."

—*Thomas A. Edison*

Agile means quick with ease. Can we achieve a goal of learning any subject in an agile way? The answer is yes. Agile way of learning creates an interest. As mentioned in an earlier chapter, interest helps us to focus on anything as our mind perceives the learning quicker. Let's take the case of mathematics to implement the agile way to learn it easily.

Creating mathematics table using agile way

Tables are base for mathematics. Memorising mathematics tables during school days has been a laborious task for all but a few, who knew the technique of creating them quickly – or, in other words, who knew the agile way to create them. Let's learn the agile way to create tables between 12 to 99 quickly.

You can use this technique for creating any table between 12 and 99. Let's create the table for 32.

Steps to create the table for 32:

1. Write down the table.

    Draw the one line below that table.

    Write down the same table again, as shown below.

    32
    ___

    32

    Now take the value from the unit's place of the upper row (2) and add it to the one from the unit's place of the lower row (2).

2. Write down this 4 just below the 2 of the lower row (or just below the unit's place of the lower row).

$$\begin{array}{r} 32 \\ \hline 32 \\ 4 \end{array}$$

3. Now keep on adding unit's values (2) from the upper row with the resulting numbers (4). The next rows will be 2+4= 6, 2+6=8…

$$\begin{array}{r} 32 \\ \hline 32 \\ 4 \\ 6 \\ 8 \end{array}$$

4. If the total value of above addition is resulted in double digit number, then you have to write down or take the unit's value from that total. Here the next answer is 2+8=10 (two digits), so we have to take the unit's value from this double-digit figure 10 (0), write it just below the 8 and put a dot in front (as shown below). You are going to add this dot as one while doing the same addition with ten place on left side.

$$\begin{array}{r} 32 \\ \hline 32 \\ 4 \\ 6 \\ 8 \\ .0 \end{array}$$

5. As you have to keep on adding one value from upper side table in resulting answer (here 0). The next row will read 2+0= 2.

$$
\begin{array}{r}
32 \\
\hline
32 \\
4 \\
\mathbf{6} \\
\mathbf{8} \\
\mathbf{.0} \\
\mathbf{2}
\end{array}
$$

6. Keep on repeating the same till the time you get the answer 0 at tenth. As shown below

$$
\begin{array}{r}
32 \\
\hline
32 \\
4 \\
\mathbf{6} \\
\mathbf{8}
\end{array}
$$

.0 ←**Write down the unit value from double-digit answer (10) and put a dot in front (0 is unit value here)**

$$
\begin{array}{r}
\mathbf{2} \\
\mathbf{4} \\
\mathbf{6} \\
\mathbf{8}
\end{array}
$$

.0 ←**Write down the unit value from double-digit answer (10) and put a dot in front (0 is unit value here)**

7. Next, keep on adding to the ten's place in an identical way. Don't forget to add a dot as one while doing this.

Adding ten's value- $3+3=6, 3+6=9, 3+9=12, 3+12=15+1=16$ (We have added 1 as dot's value at the fifth), $3+16=19$, $3+19=22$, $3+22=25$, $3+25=28$, $3+28=31+1=32$ (We have added 1 as dot's value at the tenth)

$$\frac{32}{}$$

32

64

96

128

16.0 ← (We have added 1 as dot's value in resulting answer of 15, thus 15+1=16)

192

224

256

288

32.0 ← (We have added 1 as dot's value in resulting answer of 31, thus 31+1=32)

Finally, our table for 32 is ready. You can create any table between 12-99 using this agile way technique. This is just one example: implementing many such techniques in learning is called agile learning (or quick and easy learning). Many students prefer to learn this way as compared to old rote method of learning.

How to find Agile way to solve mathematical questions?

If we solve the mathematics problems quickly and easily using core formulae, such formulae can be called agile formulae. It's like finding a flexible frame that adjusts according to photo size. Core math formulae are like flexible frames that adjust to solve any problem related to that chapter. For example, Profit and Loss in Grade 5 level mathematics has the following core formulae to solve any question from that chapter and are called as agile formulas.

Profit = Selling Price – Cost Price or **P= SP – CP**

Loss = Cost Price – Selling Price or **L= CP – SP**

As mentioned in an earlier chapter, we prefer to learn topics vertically when compared to horizontally. Subjects like mathematics are best to suited to convert questions into vertical column.

Take values form horizontal questions and put them into vertical columns to solve them quickly using above mentioned agile formulae of profit and loss.

Ques. No.	*Cost Price (CP)*	*Selling Price (SP)*	*Profit (P)*	*Loss (L)*
1	800	_ _ _? _ _ _	218	_ _ ? _ _ _ _
2	_ _ ? _ _ _	250	_ _ ? _ _ _	50

The problems are easy and quick to solve by putting the values provided in the above table (profit, loss, selling price or cost price) and using profit and loss formulae.

Let's solve the question no. 1 of the table.

P = SP – CP

218 = SP – 800

$218 + 800 = SP$

$1018 = SP$

Therefore, Selling Price (SP) = 1018

The profit is already mentioned. Thus, loss will be 0 (or use profit formulae to solve above question as profit is already mentioned)

Let's solve the question no. 2.

$L = CP - SP$

$50 = CP - 250$

$50 + 250 = CP$

$300 = CP$

Therefore, cost price (CP) is 300

The loss is already mentioned. Thus, profit would be 0 (or used loss formulae to solve above question as loss is already mentioned)

Following is the resulting answer of above table after applying loss and profit agile formulas:

Sr. No.	Cost Price	Selling Price	Profit	Loss
1	800	_ _ _1018_ _ _	218	_ _0_ _ __
2	_ _ 300_ _ __	250	_ _ 0_ _ __	50

Applying method like this is called as agile way of learning, where agile formulae or methods are used for set frame of problems consistently. The purpose of this chapter is to make you aware about the use of agile way in subjects like mathematics.

CHAPTER
Fourteen

Leverage in Learning

"When we leverage, we aggregate and organize existing resources to achieve success."

—**Richie Norton**

Achieving more with less time or effort is called leverage. For example, if a person earns Rs 45,000 per month. If she earns ten times of that amount (i.e. Rs 450,000) in a particular month, then she has leveraged her time against the earning. This is called as leverage in earning. We will discuss about how to achieve leverage in learning in this chapter.

How to achieve more with less time and effort?

In a similar way if you are learning more by putting less time and effort is called as leverage in learning. Here one can apply different learning techniques like mind map, agile way, converting the content into vertical form and flow charts or by converting chapters into stories, applying the different senses to remember the content etc. All these play important roles in leverage in learning and help anyone to achieve more with less time and efforts.

Applying 80/20 Principle to learning

One can observe the 80/20 Principle everywhere around us. For example, 80% of wealth is held by 20% of people; 20% employees in a company yield 80% of profit; if you are running 10 companies, two will always yield 80% profit. If you have been preparing ten questions of a chapter, two will be the most important and probably will appear in the exam. This is called the 80/20 Principle or Riddle. Find out this effective 20% and leverage your time and effort towards it or find out these two important questions of a chapter and prioritise them while preparing for the exam. Leverage your efforts towards the important 20%.

Giving break in Learning Slot

On an average a person can concentrate for just 30 minutes in a stretch. After that her concentration level drops. You may have observed that your child couldn't learn as per your expectation even though she had been learning continuously for the past two hours. The reason is that she had been mindful and focused only for the first 30 minutes and was unable to concentrate after that.

To overcome this problem, you need to allow her to take a five-minute break every 30 minutes. During these five minutes, she can do something other than studying, for example, watch one of her favourite songs, solve a puzzle, or take a leisure walk. Let's compare the concentration level with energy drink bottle. The level of concentration is proportionate to level of energy drink available in the bottle and that drink last for 30 minutes only. You have to take a five-minute break to refill the bottle. Her concentration level will pick up again after this break. Thus, every two-hour slot of learning (120 minutes) should have four five-minute intervals (total 20 minutes). Now she has 100 minutes of mindful learning. Such leverage will help her study more in less time.

CHAPTER
Fifteen

Textual Character Comes Alive

"A passion for the dramatic art is inherent in
the nature of man."

—Edwin Forrest

"Textual character comes alive" involves converting textual content into drama and asking students to act in it. Teaching literature (*The Merchant of Venice* or *Julius Caesar*, for example), through drama, is an effective way of learning or teaching. Teachers can conduct annual "Textual character comes alive" activity, where interested participants will play characters from above mentioned literature or use them as an annual day topic for drama.

Learning will be fun through an act. Impact of learning will also be more, as students will have storylines and will use dialogue, character emotions, and costumes of that era. They will never forget the experience. The textual character comes alive activity uses all major senses like auditory and visual senses by watching a live act, and kinaesthetic senses by acting and hand gestures.

This activity mainly involves:

1. Selecting the literature topic

2. Character Screening

3. Dialogue and character assigning

4. Ask participant to act or play the role of selected character (for 5 or 10 minutes)

5. Judge the best play or character

6. Announce the winner

All the students and participants watch the performances in the auditorium along with the judges and teachers. Teaching literature through an act by and for students is one of the best ways of learning. Teachers act as mediators. They facilitate the activity and accomplishes the learning goal.

Imagine the impact of learning by students who witnesses dialogues, characters and sequences of an act unfolding in front of them one by one. It's almost a permanent imprint of literature on their mind.

Conclusion

Schools and colleges in India have certain frames of working or methods for teaching and learning. These are passed on from one generation to the next. These frames need drastic changes. Many countries spend significant portions of their GDP on education to tap the potential of their population. Technology has become part of their teaching and learning. Here in India, forget technology, we don't have proper toilet facilities for our students. Learning potentials are vast in both rural and urban areas. Farming is still considered a job of the illiterate. No one considers combining farming with education. The educated rural are moving to urban areas, while the uneducated rural population are left behind with small pieces of farmland and scarcity of water, which is killing them. This large population is yet to realise their potential.

GDP of USA is 20,220 billion USD, whereas the GDP of India is 2,900 billion USD (source: Google). It indicates that we are yet to tap the rural population who are left behind due to non-education. This can be resolved by providing quality education at all levels. Make the education accessible, affordable and subsidise it heavily. Open learning or skill centres at village level. Use scientific methods in learning. The base of learning has to be inseminated in them with structured programmes. The education sector will open a lot of jobs itself.

We have seen the first- and second-generation people who had moved out from villages and settled down to urban areas to make the cities flourish. We have developed transport and communication technologies and made them accessible to everyone. Unfortunately, availing quality education is still out of reach for marginalised poor in India.

During the 1980s, government school were overflowing with students which needed to be tapped, streamlined and structured, but they were left for chaos, as teachers had to manage a large number of students in a single class which resulted in degradation of quality education. The influx was so high that they denied admission to extra students (in an earlier chapter story titled Hindi Medium is based on a true story of denying admission in school). Poverty and poor teaching methods led to students leaving the school after failing repeatedly. This created opportunities for small private schools. The early 1990s witnessed parents moving their children from government to private schools. Private school started to flourish everywhere in cities with minimum available resources. They provided superior education compared to the government schools. Poor marginalised students were left to government schools.

This book is a small part of this big make-up and an attempt to make you aware about various learning skills in easy and simple ways. Picking up one chapter at a time and implementing it on daily basis will enrich your learning experience. We need to add a lot of scientific ways in learning. We need many experts to speed up this process. We always discussed that the education sector required a lot of changes, but it is hard to realise exactly what changes we are looking for.

We have made an attempt to list these changes of teaching and learning through this book and are based on various methods implemented in class learning of one of the top ten ICSE school of Mumbai, India. This school provides admission to poor marginalised students through RTE Act (Right To Education Act). We can fill this gap by opening up more educational institutions like this and saturate the gap between the rich and the poor by providing quality education. To fill this gap fast, I urge you to sponsor the education of one poor child as it will make a big impact in the development of our country.

References

Allen, David (2001). *Getting Things Done: The Art of Stress-free Productivity*, London, UK: Piatkus.

Assaraf, John (2008). *The Answer: Grow Any Business, Achieve Financial Freedom, and Live an Extraordinary Life.* New York, USA: Crown Business. Atria Books.

Buzan, Tony (2002). *How to Mind Map: The Ultimate Thinking Tool That Will Change Your Life*, UK: Thorsons.

Canfield, Jack (2011). *The Power of Focus: How to Hit Your Business, Personal and Financial Targets with Confidence and Certainty.* USA: Vermillion.

Carey, Benedict (2014). *How We Learn: Throw out the rule book and unlock your brain's potential.* London, UK: Macmillan.

Dweck, Carol (2006). *Mindset: The New Psychology of Success.* New York, USA: Robinson.

Harari, Yuval Noah (2011). *Sapiens: A Brief History of Humankind.* London, UK: Penguin Random House.

Hedges, Burk (1999). *Read & Grow Rich: How the Hidden Power of Reading Can Make You Richer in All Areas of Your Life.* USA: I N T I Pub & Resource Books Inc.

Koch, Richard (2008). *The 80/20 Principle: The Secret to Achieving More with Less.* New York, USA: Crown Business.

Mccullough, Joe (2014). *Accelerated Learning Techniques for Students: Learn More in Less Time,* UK: Createspace Independent Pub.